SAINT BENEDICT'S RULE FOR FAIR PLAY IN SPORTS

Being an imagined guide by the 6th Century
founder of Western monasticism for
21st Century athletes, coaches, and fans

First Printing

The athletic departments of
the College of Saint Benedict and Saint John's University
receive all proceeds from their sales of this book.

Grateful acknowledgment to
Little & Company, Minneapolis,
for design.

ISBN 13: 978-0-615-15253-0

*For the teachers and coaches
who give so unselfishly to
develop the next generation of leaders*

The Rule

Prologue: What Are "Sports" For?

Benedict, son of a Roman noble, is born about A.D. 480 during a century of invasions, earthquakes, plague, famine, and the last of the Western Roman emperors. He spends his boyhood in Rome, lives with his parents, attends school, but then drops out.

"Giving over his books, and forsaking his father's house and wealth, with a mind only to serve God," wrote Saint Gregory the Great, "he sought for some place where he might attain to the desire of his holy purpose." That place turns out to be a cave near Subiaco, about thirty miles east of Rome, where Benedict lives in seclusion as a hermit. Some years later he founds a monastery on a mountain above Cassino, about eighty miles south of Rome.

It is there he writes his "little rule for beginners," an owner's manual for a monastic community tempered with his generous understanding of human nature and framed by the values of humility, community, stability, equality, frugality, and the dignity of work and prayer. Benedict dies in about A.D. 547 and his Rule becomes one of the cultural underpinnings of Western civilization, but let's ...

… imagine for a moment: Benedict has come back. He wants to complete the education he abandoned in 6th Century Rome, and he is with us today at the College of Saint Benedict and Saint John's University in Minnesota. He is a sophomore major in biology, an exchange student from Norcia, Umbria (Italy). He is a diligent scholar, but perhaps struggles with microbiology.

After a while on our campuses he senses that, essential as they are, spirituality and scholarship are not enough — for God has given young Benedict a body. Careful observer, he notes the importance of "sports" in student life and secular culture — indeed, how much of it strikes him as a secular religion with its dogmas, community of believers, rituals and rites, its pantheon of heroes. Careful listener, he hears the sports lingo that sprinkles our language: *Hey, that's a layup; it's a slam dunk; he struck out on that one; it just came out of left field; just give me a ballpark estimate; the ball's in your court; three yards and a cloud of dust; she dropped the ball; all we want is a level playing field.*

He counts more pages for sports in newspapers than for any other subject. He sees that attendance at sports events exceeds that at churches, synagogues, and mosques. ESPN sports every hour of the day. Sports facilities that occupy more square feet on some campuses than any other endeavor. As much space in some campus bookstores for sports "affinity" apparel as for books. He wanders down to our football, baseball, and soccer fields and gazes in awe at the manicured pastures of gridiron (imitation grass!), diamond, and pitch. He puzzles over the obsession with fantasy leagues and March Madness. He marvels: The nation's most storied college football team is named after the Blessed Virgin and has a "Touchdown Jesus." He reads of great women athletes — Babe Didrikson Zaharias, Gertrude Ederle, Sonja Henie, Wilma Rudolph, Billie Jean King, Jackie Joyner-Kersee, Mia Hamm — and he's amazed at the progress for equal opportunity for girls and women in high school and college sports, thanks be to God (and the late Congresswoman Patsy Mink, Hawaii) for Title IX.

In a halogen-lit carrel in the library through the night, he scours modern American literature to try to make some sense of America's sports culture: Bernard Malamud's *The Natural*, W. P. Kinsella's *Shoeless Joe*, Roger Kahn's *The Boys of Summer*, George Plimpton's *Paper Lion*, Lauren Hillenbrand's *Seabiscuit*, and (we are partial) Austin Murphy's *The Sweet Season*. He rents DVDs of *Pride of the Yankees*, *Knute Rockne: All American*, *Fear Strikes Out*, *Chariots of Fire*, *Hoop Dreams*, *Hoosiers*, *Miracle on Ice*, *Rudy*, *A League of Their Own*, *Saint Ralph*, *Bend It Like Beckham*, and *We Are Marshall*. He takes issue with his fellow Italian, the great Lombardi, about winning being the only thing, what Christopher Lasch called the "cult of victory." Instead, he is justifiably proud of the coaching philosophy of another fellow countryman, the even greater Gagliardi.

He asks himself fundamental questions about the nature and attraction of sports to try to decipher the value of an activity that from his Sixth Century experience, appears to have no connection with either *ora* (worship) or *labora* (work) and, moreover, seems to have no utility at all. It does not seem to provide the community with any useful good or service. Did a double play ever feed the hungry, a three-pointer clothe the naked, a touchdown heal the sick? At least music, painting, and sculpture can be employed in the sacred arts to praise God, but what exactly is the social *benefit* of sports? Indeed, social *penalty*. The average fan can afford seven-dollar nosebleed seats at a Major League Baseball game, but

Benedict can't grasp the extravagance of some pro sports fans. Can the most expensive courtside ticket for the Los Angeles Lakers really be $2,300 a *game*?

He finds on the Web random scraps of information, some cynical, some moralistic, that shape his view of the value and ethics of sports. He happens upon a 1923 poem, *Alumnus Football*, by Grantland Rice, myth-making sportswriter of the early 20th Century. Did anyone then, he wonders, really believe its quaint couplets? Does anyone believe them in today's "nothing matters but the W" culture?

"For when the One Great Scorer comes
To write against your name,
He marks — not that you won or lost —
But how you played the game."

He finds a quote attributed to Glenn Dobbs, an All-American football player at the University of Tulsa in the 1940s, who summed up the that's-for-sissies view: "If you spend a lot of time on sportsmanship, you're going to spend a lot of time losing." Recent examples show

Benedict how blurred the ethical line is between what's fair and foul. Was it fair play for Alex Rodriguez of the New York Yankees to shout while rounding third and distract the third baseman into letting a pop-up drop, eventually causing three runs to score — or when he swatted the ball away from the glove of the pitcher trying to tag him out at first? How about in the women's 1999 World Cup soccer final when goalkeeper Briana Scurry illegally, and openly, moved forward to cut down the angle to block the decisive shot against China and win the title for the United States?

But there's hope. He watches a replay of the fourth round of the Australian Open from January 2001. France's Sebastian Grosjean, seeded 16th in the world, is up two sets to one over Sweden's Magnus Norman, seeded fourth. Grosjean's first serve, his third match point, appears to be an ace. Norman walks to the net to concede victory to Grosjean, but the chair umpire runs onto the court and says Grosjean's serve nicked the net and Grosjean should serve again. Norman refuses. The match, he says, is over. "I did not think there had been a let," says Norman. "If I had taken it and the match had turned around, I'm not sure I could have gone home feeling good about myself."

Benedict reflects: Mr. Norman's gesture certainly is noble, truly the heart of "sportsmanship" (graciousness in victory or defeat). But our young Benedict opts for a much broader concept, closer to the Greek ideal, to sum up his personal creed for sports: "fair play," how ethical standards for sports are integrated into one's whole life, on *and* off the field of play, not just for athletes but for all involved in sports: coaches and teachers, staff, spectators, governing bodies, journalists, marketers. He uses "play" in its original Greek sense (*paizein*, to play; *pais*, child) — he sees sports as what they really are: children's games that adults take seriously; games not intended as an end in themselves but for learning life lessons, as handed down to 21st Century America by Victorian England's public schools of the 19th Century.

With Latin his vernacular, he sees that "sport" (*desporto*, Latin, to carry away) can "trans-port" us to another world. But, he asks, is that all there is to this? What's the purpose of these games in an academic setting? Entertainment? Diversion? If these are just "sports," he thinks, then the national governing body should rename itself the NCSA, the National Collegiate

Sports Association. Benedict uses "sports" in the title of his thesis because it's the word he hears in daily conversation. He prefers, more precisely, "athletics" because it at least, he believes, has a worthy goal, the pursuit of a "prize." This is the athletic context in which he reads the famous line from Tennyson's *Ulysses*: "To strive, to seek, to find, and not to yield."

Seeing the Athlete in the Sixth Century Rule

There are hints of an athletic temperament in Benedict's Rule. The Sixth Century Benedict may have had the look of an athlete — not rotund and lethargic in the monkish stereotype, but the product of a frugal diet and hardy constitution: lean, muscular, sinewy, perhaps a spring in his step. He appreciated and cared for the condition and strength of his body (in harmony with his mind) as an instrument of God. He moderated its use, honored the dignity of physical exertion. He knew that to follow his Rule, one must not be just spiritually fit but physically fit. He saw exercise as a gift from God, the noble "re-creation" of the human spirit in God's name. A student of the Old Testament, he surely thrilled to its heroic athletic stories: David downs Goliath (he shoots, he scores!); Jonah's three-day walk across Nineveh (what endurance!); Samson dispatches the Philistines with the jawbone of an ass (what a comeback!). He found solace in Isaiah 40:31, that those who hope in the Lord "will run and not grow weary"; and in Zechariah 8:5, "And the streets of the city will be filled with boys and girls playing in its streets." He saw the sports of his Sixth Century Rome as evil diversions, but his original Rule also is replete with references — "while we are still in our bodies" — to personal discipline, self-denial, perseverance, the need to have "our loins girded" and to "prepare our hearts and our bodies to do battle under the holy obedience of his commands" — all traits of an athlete in training.

Perhaps he was influenced by the great St. Basil who, preceding him by a century-and-a-half, believed a monastic community to be a "stadium in which athletes are exercised. … Its end is the glory of God according to the commandments of God."

For Sixth Century Benedict, physical exertion had a spiritual purpose: "If we wish to dwell in the tent of that kingdom, we must run to it by good deeds or we shall never reach it." He may have known the young Plato was a champion wrestler and that Plato's philosopher kings were encouraged to engage in sports as one way to build courage, valor, fortitude, discipline, self knowledge, piety, and temperance — all packaged in the Greek *arête*. He may have known the religious origins of games in ancient Greece and that the Greeks organized their games for the competitors, but Rome exploited athletic contests as public entertainment. With that profane Roman model in mind, he probably agrees with *New York Times* sportswriter Harvey Araton that a disturbing portion of commercial sports today has become "a profit- and greed-driven system that drains the joy and civility from our games."*

He certainly appreciated the spirit and physical energy of Saint Paul, who encountered stadia everywhere he went — not just in Rome, but in Tarsus, Ephesus, and Corinth — and who had the stamina of today's ultra-marathoners:

---

*True, perhaps, but not a new insight. In the 1920s, Grantland Rice was writing of highly paid sports celebrities (whose reputations he helped build): "Money to the left of them and money to the right. Money everywhere they turn from morning to the night. Only two things count at all from mountain to the sea. Part of it's percentage, and the rest is guarantee."

"Do you not know that in a race all the runners run, but only one gets the prize? Run in such a way as to get the prize" (1 Corinthians 9:24); "Therefore I do not run like a man running aimlessly; I do not fight like a man beating the air" (1 Corinthians 9:26); "that I may boast on the day of Christ that I did not run or labor for nothing" (Philippians 2:16); "let us run with perseverance the race marked out for us" (Hebrews 12:1); "You were running a good race. Who cut in on you and kept you from obeying the truth?" (Galatians 5:7).

Young Benedict: the Athlete Today

We can easily see young Benedict today as a natural athlete (*athlein*, Greek, to contend for a prize; *athlon*, prize), not a varsity star but one of those smaller, gritty, intense types in intramurals, club sports, and pickup games. Maybe a basketball point guard who scores only five or six points a game but plays tenacious defense. Maybe a wrestler. Surely, someday a player-coach. He admires the creativity, concentration, exuberance, and agony of the athlete in competition, the choreographic beauty of a well-executed play, or the simple joy of a solitary, brisk walk or run in the woods — all of it, as Aristotle said, to free the spirit and ennoble the soul.

He has special empathy for his classmates, female and male alike, who regard themselves as klutzes, who feel excluded from the fields of sport. But he would not let them off the hook. Remembering the Greek goddess of victory, "fair-ankled" Nike, he would implore them: "Just do *some*thing. Lace 'em up! Walk! Run! Bike! Swim! Climb! Ski! God gave you a body. Just do it!"

Despite what his Rule says about the absolute necessity for silence on the monastic grounds, I see him (as I've seen hundreds of Benedictines of both genders over the decades) as a fan in the stands at, say, a Saint Benedict's basketball game, ever loyal to his community and team, barely able to conceal his frustration over the injustice of a referee's call. To himself through his teeth: *Hey ref, she's all over her!*

He sees how the spirit and character of an athletic team emerge from the spirit and character of a community — especially in the contemplative, countercultural settings of our two campuses "away from the world." He equates the "dignity of exercise" on the field with the "dignity of work" in the field. He sees the work in play and the play in work — the good sweat common to both. He lingers over the recollection of Johnnies' hockey in the 1930s by the late Senator Eugene McCarthy (SJU, '35): "The exultation of a goal, and of victory, with players near exhaustion, muscles aching, lungs burning, and then the sweat cooling against the body, under wool, while the will waits for new strength to undress, to shower, to return to humanity — the players like reluctant centaurs having to put off the horse half, and become men again."

He carefully notes, as many have, similarities in ritual and liturgy between religious services and athletic contests. He sees uniforms as a form of vestment. The solemn stride of the helmet-less captains to the center of the football field for the rite of the coin toss. The two-line layup and rebound drill in basketball warm-ups. Baseball's "sacrifice" fly. The ritualistic gathering of hockey and soccer teams around their goalies before play begins.

He sees many aspects of major college and professional sports as "ludicrous" — from the ludi (*ludus*, Latin, game or play) of his Roman boyhood — the vulgar, violent chariot races, gladiator contests, and animal hunts dedicated to pagan gods in Roman arenas. At the Division III level of intercollegiate sports, however, he catches the spirit of school "fight" songs — sees "fight" not as intent to do physical harm (as George Orwell saw soccer: a "species of fighting") but as the "fight" against evil ways, as in his militant metaphors "armed from the ranks," "solitary combat," and "to fight single-handed." Tracing back 600 years before Christ, he finds threads of wisdom in Lao Tzu's classic *Tao Te Ching* that appear in the fabric of his Sixth Century Rule. Athletes coping with fatigue, tension, and anxiety can benefit from this ancient "fair play" wisdom today: yielding not rigid, rhythmic not mechanical, assertive (like water) not aggressive with force, focusing on how the game is played not the score, encouraging others not trying to dominate them. "They succeed and do not boast," says the *Tao Te Ching*; "They succeed and do not make claims." He is wary of excessive competition in athletics just as he was wary in the Sixth Century of overly austere monks who competed for blue ribbons in spirituality.

So, does Benedict today see an important role for exercise and sports in *ora et labora* and in living a good life? I believe he does. He sides with Michael Novak in *The Joy of Sports* that sports have become the "chief civilizing agent" in our society. He agrees with philosopher Arthur Holmes (Wheaton College, Ill.), who wrote in *Contours of a World View* that play should be seen not as on the fringe of our lives but central to our lives, as an act of worship: "It is the religious meaning of life that gives purpose and meaning to both work and play. A responsible relationship to God includes play." Benedict understands why the philosopher Albert Camus said that sports gave him his only "lessons in ethics."

Imagine Benedict now a college senior. With his penchant for codifying ideal behavior into a Rule (or regimen), and after his careful observation of how we conduct ourselves at sports events in the 21st Century, he writes his senior thesis on how to integrate worship, work, and play. What would he say through the lens of his 1,500-year-old Rule?

Many words or phrases quoted in the following text are from *Saint Benedict's Rule for Monasteries* (translated from the Latin by Leonard J. Doyle, The Liturgical Press, Saint John's Abbey, Collegeville, Minn., 1948) — the coffee-stained copy I've had for almost 50 years since acquiring it as a Saint John's Prep student. My thanks to those whose reflections begin each chapter, athletes from games past speaking to athletes today: German professor, retired *Fortune 200* corporate executive, retired insurance executive, social service manager, emergency room physician, physical education director, minor league hockey goalie, Air Force major, high school football coach, medical student, clinical psychologist, and probation officer. This Rule is guided by Benedictine values but represents the author's views only, not necessarily those of our schools.

So, daughters and sons, please "incline the ear of your heart" to the good word (*bene dicto*) on fair play in sports from our reincarnated visitor from the Sixth Century — for these words are addressed not just to athletes and coaches but to you up there in Section C, Row 24, seats five and six.

Larry Haeg
Trustee, College of Saint Benedict
Saint John's University, Class of 1967

"As a runner at Saint John's, I learned what counts is not just the outcome of the athletic event but the entire process of preparing — the discipline of training that leads to the thrill of competing. All of it happened within a community of students, most of whom got to know each other by playing some sort of sport. As part of my class work I spent a month to learn what it was like to live as a monk, and I discovered similarities between the Rule and sports. I found meditative qualities in the daily routine of stretching, running, recovery, weight room training, a run in the backwoods, and how it connected body and spirit."

Dr. Daniel Kramer
SJU, 1989

I.
We Search for God

We acknowledge the primacy of God and look for God
in the ordinary events of each day.

"We believe that the divine presence is everywhere."
RB 19.1

Sports can be a "sacrament." It can have a sacred purpose, be a spiritual journey, an opportunity to seek God. The fields, courts, and rinks on which we play and the spectators who observe us are part of a "school for the service of the Lord." For as Jacob said, "Surely the Lord is in this place — and I did not know it!" (Genesis 28:16). The grace of God is present in our training, self-denial, discipline, teamwork, on the field in the contest itself, in victory and defeat. The satisfaction we get from athletics comes from God. Likewise, the ability of athletes "cannot come from themselves and must be from God."

This is more than just a game, it is an extension of academics, part of the curriculum and classroom, to prepare young women and young men to contribute to the well-being of society. We celebrate the stories of great athletic accomplishment, but we know the applause and cheers are but a vapor. Years pass; players' names, final scores, achievements, and honors are forgotten. Trophies gather dust. All that matters is the spirit with which the game is played.

Fair play as an acquired habit

The spirit of fair play, which makes us aware of God's presence, is cultivated by habits acquired over time with practice. Athletics is a means to an end, not an end in itself. It is for the "cultivation of virtue." (Saint Paul calls it "proven character." Romans 5:1–5) A sport is not just a series of physical actions or "plays" but an attitude of the mind and spirit. It has much in common with art, drama, or dance. All eyes are on the athlete as a performer on a stage, fully in the moment, as in worship or work.

Religious symbols in sports

When an athlete makes the Sign of the Cross on the field or points heavenward after a well-executed play, the gesture should be seen as thanksgiving for the gift of the game, not asking God for victory. Not by accident is prayer so pervasive in sports, as in football's "Hail Mary" pass or "immaculate reception." We do not attribute them to divine intervention, but so-called "miracle" plays inspire us, such as Gene Sarazen's 225-yard double eagle with a four wood en route to winning the 1935 Masters or the 1980 victory by the United States over the Soviet Union ("Do you believe in miracles?") in men's Olympic hockey.

Prayer before and after a game

When a team prays, let it be for the opportunity to compete, for the joy and beauty of the game, and that all players be spared injury.

Thank you God for the —
Gift of our bodies —
muscle, tendon, skill, and strength.
Gift of our spirit —
discipline, courage, the will to win.
Camaraderie of this team —
trust, respect, support, and care.
For all who make this game possible — seen and unseen.
Amen!

"It was true more than 40 years ago, and I hope it's true today. Our teams were part of the community, not separate. I don't recall any sports cliques. Many members of our teams were on the dean's list and went on to get advanced degrees. The football team had its lockers in the old gym, and when we emerged from the gym in our red-and-white uniforms, we walked across campus to the stadium accompanied by hundreds of students who walked with us. We were all one student body."

Joe Mucha
SJU, 1966

II.
Community Living

We form stable relationships in the community — becoming who we are by our relationships with others.

"… and may he bring us all together to everlasting life."
RB 72.12

The joy of sports, like worship and work, should be integrated into our community, not segregated from it.

Sports as "of" the community

Athletic teams and those who support them are of our community and represent our community to the world beyond our campuses.

Athletes should not regard themselves as superior to non-athletes, or be housed in separate dorms or eat meals apart from the community like mercenaries, but be integrated into our communities. At the common table. On the common field. In the common classroom. In common worship.

Serving each others' needs

Since "all exaltation is a kind of pride," all team members should renounce their individual will for the good of the team (the community). No individual — "puffed up with any pride" — can take sole credit for a team achievement. The entire team shares in the contributions of each of its players. Everyone on the team can contribute regardless of talent or skill.

"No one is to pursue what he judges better for himself; but instead, what he judges better for someone else" on the team. All players "should by turn serve one another's needs" and consider themselves "lower and of less account than anyone else" on the team.

No special privileges for athletes

Students who are athletes should choose to enroll in our schools for academics, not athletics. The student's performance in the classroom is more important than on the field. The term "student-athlete" is to be earned by the student, not bestowed generically. Student-athletes should submit to the same academic discipline as all other students.

Sharing resources

All members of the team share equally in the school's resources as members of one community — so all sports equipment is community property, not property of the athletes. All on the field of play receive an inheritance from those who preceded them. Thus there is, to paraphrase historian David McCullough, no such person as a self-made athlete. Each is endowed, developed, enriched by innumerable benefactors known and unknown.

All students part of the team in spirit

Those who don't make the team should accept the decision with grace. Don't wallow in it. Redouble your effort to earn a place on the team next season, or channel your energy into something more suited to your skill and talent. This Rule could have an endless list of the famous and obscure denied a starting position or even a jersey number on a team roster and who persisted to develop their talent in that sport, another sport or some entirely different endeavor. A student cut from the team should stay a part of the team in spirit.

"The Benedictine spirit of care for the individual, of love and forgiveness, seemed to pervade the campus. It influenced the way we played sports. It translated into deep pride for the team and for the university we represented; not wanting to let the team down, giving it your all every game. These values came to life for me through great counselors such as Father Adelard and athletic director George Durenberger. I remember long walks with Adelard, and the time when I was a student and he was in his late 40s when he bet me he could beat me in a foot race on the football field if I gave him a 10-yard lead. He tucked his cassock inside his belt and off we went. Anything more than a 10-yard lead and he would have beaten me."

Jim Lehman
SJU, 1956

III.
Taking Counsel

We call the community together to counsel for decisions — to be
rooted, to share our mission, to stand firm in our promises.

*"As often as anything important is to be done ... the abbot shall call the
whole community together and explain what the business is ..."*
RB 3.1

The team, as a community, should be open to counsel. All players on the team can benefit from counsel of others on the team and should be open to it regardless of seniority. Just as the prioress and abbot call their monastic communities together, so do coaches call the team together. For "important business" the coach may call together the entire team because "the Lord often reveals to the younger what is best."

Respect for young and old

Respect should be accorded more senior members of the team for their experience and wisdom, but younger players should be given every opportunity to display their talent, and thus "absolutely nowhere shall age automatically determine rank" on the field of play.

Conduct at team meetings

Team practices and team meetings are a way to do "everything with counsel." Players, like monks and sisters, should "be ready to arise without delay when the signal is given."

Coaches: Avoid harsh criticism of a player's performance in the presence of the rest of the team, but rather admonish the player "secretly at first."

The role of captains

The team chooses captains not just for their physical ability but their leadership skills. Because they are in the action on the field, unlike the coach who watches from the distant sideline, they should carefully observe how the team works as a whole, give counsel when needed, and mediate disputes fairly. They should see that the more junior players are treated with respect.

Community counsel

Athletic facilities on our campuses are not isolated, self-contained enterprises. "Physical" education is integrated into the rest of our curriculum and connected to every other discipline in our liberal arts, such as anthropology, biology, chemistry, physics, psychology, and sociology. Therefore, the broader community should be consulted for important decisions on athletics that have effect beyond athletes and coaches, such as in which sports a school should compete "outside the walls" or "inside the walls" (see page 93), and the location, size, and amenities of facilities.

Light and learning

A famous example of "community counsel" occurred at the University of Chicago in the late 1930s. Its young president, Robert Hutchins, began a debate among students, faculty, the board, and the community that led to dropping intercollegiate football at the school, home of Amos Alonzo Stagg and Jay Berwanger, the first Heisman trophy winner. Hutchins favored "the urge to play for fun and health, instead of the urge to win at any cost." He wanted to "broaden the base of athletic participation, so that all students, graduate and undergraduate, big fellows and little fellows, can play. ... The task of the colleges and universities, then, is to show the country a substitute for athleticism. That substitute is light and learning." Thirty years later, varsity football reemerged from a club sport and returned, after community counsel, to the University of Chicago at the Division III level. Light and learning prevailed.

"In his Rule, Benedict urges artisans in the community to 'practice their craft with all humility,' and not to become 'puffed up' by one's 'skillfulness.' He might have the same advice today for athletes — thou shall not grandstand. If you are good at what you do in sports, your skill will shine through; you don't have to call attention to it."

Grace Donovan, O.S.B.
CSB, 1950s

IV.
Respect for Persons

We reverence and respect each person regardless
of class, rank, culture, background, or skill.

*"No one is to pursue what is judged best for oneself,
but instead, what is better for someone else."*
RB 72.7

Sports should encourage respect for self, respect for others, and respect for the game. Behavior on the field reflects character off the field. It's been said, "Sports do not build character, they reveal it." Athletes don't blame others for their mistakes, they "take responsibility" for them.

The harm of profanity

Athletes and coaches are no different than any of us who curse to ourselves in private moments of frustration or anger. We acknowledge this weakness and try to control it. Profanity is harmful when it's public for all ears present and is done to abuse others. This includes obscene gestures, intimidation, taunting, lying, cheating, or intent to harm. In sports, it should not be a taunt for a taunt ("Return sevenfold into the bosom of our neighbors the taunts with which they taunted you." Psalm 79:12) but forgiveness ("seventy times seven," Matthew 18:21).

The conduct of the coach

Coaches should always put the well-being of their players ahead of the desire to win, be models of behavior for their players. If, for example, they don't want their players to smoke or drink, then they shouldn't smoke or drink. They should honor their promises to their players. Their comments or criticism should be directed not at the player but the player's performance.

Needless complaining

Coaches shouldn't argue repeatedly with referees or use their players as agents for whining. Constant complaining detracts from a team's focus on execution and can blind the referee to a legitimate gripe. Neither should coaches or players argue with their opponents. They should walk away from the temptation. Their complaining encourages younger coaches to mimic them — such as the Major League Baseball manager celebrated for cursing and kicking dirt at umpires and setting a record for the number of games from which umpires ejected him.

Parents as coaches

Parents (the student's first coaches) and family should put the physical and emotional welfare of their daughters and sons ahead of any personal desire to win. They should respect the coach's decision for who makes the team and who's on the field. They should see themselves as observers at their children's games just as if they were observers in a classroom.

Blessed be the benchwarmers

Those who "warm the bench" are as valuable to the team as those on the field. All members of the team are valued.

When a player is injured

Injured athletes "must be patiently borne with." When a player has fallen and is down on the field of play, it's right and good for an opponent to extend a hand — perhaps the single most symbolic gesture of fair play in sports.

When a play is completed

When a play's over, the player nearest the ball should hand it to the referee as a sign of respect.

Showing appreciation

When any athlete is injured on the field of play and is helped from the field, it's right and good for all spectators to show their appreciation for the athlete's courage. When an athlete or team makes an exceptional play, it's right and good for all spectators to show appreciation.

How the opposing team is to be thanked

When the game's over, the teams should meet on the field, the court, or the rink to congratulate one another. Opposing coaches should do the same. They should part the field as friends, so if they meet again they can look back with pride on their behavior. No greater compliment can be paid, one player to another, than to say the contest was hard fought but at all times fair.

When scoring is to be avoided

In a game in which two teams are not fairly matched in skill and talent, the coach of the better team should not run up the score but instead "empty the bench" as much as possible.

Mutual respect: women and men

Women and men, you are kin in sport. Respect each other as equals on your separate fields of play. Respect the different styles of play of the sisterhood and brotherhood when you compete together. You have much to learn from each other about the value of competition, courage and determination, the will to win, compromise, teamwork, relationships, empathy, and how to endure pain and injury. Do not stereotype each other; such as the hypocrite who publicly advocates equality for women in athletics and then whispers "Nice putt, Alice" to his golfing buddy on the green, or those who engage in unfair, demeaning references to "dumb jocks."

many of us have the courage of the great baseball pitcher Sandy Koufax, who refused to pitch against the Minnesota Twins in the first game of the 1965 World Series because it fell on Yom Kippur? Indeed, others sacrificed more than Koufax, who returned to pitch two shutouts as the Dodgers won the Series. Eric Liddell *(Chariots of Fire)* chose not to compete on Sunday in the 100 meters in the 1924 Paris Olympics. Shawn Green (baseball) and Jeff Halpern (hockey) routinely do not play on Yom Kippur. Eli Herring, a 340-pound lineman with a 3.5 GPA at Brigham Young, chose to be a high school math teacher rather than play pro football on Sundays. Aleisha Cramer-Rose made the U.S. women's national soccer team at age 16 but passed up professional soccer because she could not reconcile playing on Sunday with her religious beliefs: "Everybody knows what's right for them. I'd rather follow what I believe. When you do what you feel is right, you have a peaceful feeling."

"Probably very few student-athletes at Saint Ben's or Saint John's have read the Rule of Saint Benedict, and I'm sure none of them thinks about it before, during, or after a game. But it's amazing how many of them conduct themselves in sports in a way that models Benedict's values. That's a miracle of sorts; I don't know how it happens. Maybe it's the little things we do — such as treating every spectator to free ice cream at a Saint Ben's home game when we win in basketball. It brings everyone together after the game, the hosts and our guests, to enjoy each other's company."

Margaret Hughes
CSB, 1960s

VI.
Hospitality

We practice hospitality and respect for all persons;
welcome with warmth, acceptance, and joy.

"Let all ... be received as Christ."
RB 53.1

Both teams should bring out the best in each other, not as enemies but partners, for without the opponent there would be no game. Athletes should compete with intensity and determination, but they should have a generous spirit toward their opponents. Both teams learn from each other how to perform better on the field.

Let all welcome all

Visiting teams and fans should be welcomed as guests in our homes, greeted as we would want to be greeted as visitors to their campus by all who serve as modern-day porters: parking attendants, ticket sellers, concessionaires, groundskeepers, public address announcers. After the game, if possible, let us worship God together and give thanks for the gift of sport and community.

The behavior of spectators

Spectators: Enjoy the game but beware, "fan" is from *fanaticus* (from a deity, frenzied; Latin) and *fanum* (temple, Latin); in other words, inspired by a false god. Don't harass the visiting team — heckling is a form of cheating. Don't intrude on the field of play or interfere with athletes on the field.

A "good word" for opponents

There should be no "evil or depraved speech" directed at players, coaches, or fans. "A good word" to them "is above the best gift." When a player errs in a game or in practice, that does not mean the player is less in God's eyes. Don't underestimate the courage, discipline, and hard work required of any athlete on the field.

How the visiting team is to be cared for

Hospitality for visiting teams should extend to the quality of their locker rooms and sideline facilities. Avoid the practice of one professional basketball coach who, though his teams often won, chose to deprive visiting teams of hot water and heat in their locker room. Depriving them of such comfort may often produce an effect opposite that desired.

"What I learned in sports at Saint John's was to play for the pure love of the game. There was never any sense of competing against anyone else on the team. We all wanted everyone to do well. We were taught to play with a quiet confidence, not to panic or worry if we lost a game. We also learned to respect the teams we played against. It all brought out the best in us. I hope we have passed all this on to the next generation of student-athletes at Saint Ben's and Saint John's."

Adam Hanna
SJU, 2006

VII.
Stewardship

We revere all creation, protecting and
perpetuating all that is good in this place.

"Regard all utensils as if they were the sacred vessels of the altar."
RB 31.10

Coaches and athletes are stewards of their schools' reputations and models of behavior for younger athletes and spectators.

Players should walk onto the field as proud stewards of the game, not as mere renters, with confidence in their team and their abilities and pride in their school but not with strutting arrogance.

Sacred vessels of sport

The material things of our games are sacred. The uniforms, helmets, pads, shoes, balls, sticks, bats, clubs, and mitts — when not excessive in cost* and when put to best use — are "sacred vessels," just like the "utensils and goods of the monastery." Likewise, we see in the green expanse of fields on which we play the life-giving energy of God, what the 12th Century abbess and visionary Hildegard of Bingen called "*O viriditas digiti Deo*" (O Life-green finger of God).

---

*Sisters and brothers: An $8,400 designer golf bag, a $2,000 titanium driver, or a $300 graphite tennis racquet are not what we have in mind when we speak of "sacred vessels of sport."

Commerce that can corrupt

Care must be taken to avoid the corrupting influence of money and commercial ventures that promote earning revenue beyond the essential needs of college programs. It is natural for schools to promote their sports to build attendance, but not so games become mere promotion for the institution.

Players are not to be "marketed" through the media as commodities to be bought or sold.

Commercial activity should not interrupt the flow of the game. Our sports are a "dot-edu" not a "dot-com."

Role of Alumnae, Alumni

Because they benefited as students, in academics and athletics, from the sacrifices of those who preceded them, likewise they should give unselfishly of their time, talent, and treasure to their alma mater ("You received without payment; give without payment"; Matthew 10:8) as befits their name (*alere*, to nourish, Latin).

They should be proud of their schools and the teams that represent them, but should not seek any undue influence, financial or otherwise, over athletics and keep academics and athletics in proper perspective.

"Sports at Saint Ben's enriched my life so much. It required me to organize my time, discipline my will, bring balance to my life, and it surrounded me with others who brought out the best in me and, I hope, vice versa. I studied with more focus because of the discipline of sports, which helped make my Air Force career possible today. I owe much of this to a chance encounter. As a high school senior, I underwent lower back surgery to correct birth defects. The hospital nurse who helped me recover was a Saint Ben's graduate. I was so impressed with her bedside manner that it was one of the reasons I chose Saint Ben's, where I pursued a nursing degree myself and where I first fully realized my God-given athletic ability."

Kathy Yarnott Lowry
CSB, 1992

VIII.
Re-creating the Whole Person

We foster an environment for re-creating the whole person.

"Through this love, all … will now begin to be observed without effort, as though naturally, for habit, … out of love for Christ, good habit, and delight in virtue."
RB 7.68–69

Every athlete wants to win. First place is the desire to excel made manifest. When gold is the prize, who seeks silver or bronze? The desire to win, however, should be not be seen as an end in itself but as the product of teamwork and disciplined preparation of mind and body. If winning is the only goal, then sport becomes an empty vessel ("molten calf," Exodus 32:4), for sport is more than entertainment, circus, diversion, amusement, wager, media coverage, bottom line, broadcast contracts, commodity bought and sold to the highest bidder in the marketplace. It is more than franchises, rankings, conference standings, win-loss records, attendance records, highlight films, first-round draft choices, playoff brackets, statistics and box scores, bragging rights, arch-rivals, apparel merchandise, gate receipts. The athlete who competes solely for the status trappings of the marketplace — that seem so important in the moment — will have "spent my strength for nothing and vanity" (Isaiah 49:4).

Questions to be asked

Our engagement in athletics — as player, coach, fan — should re-create us, make one a better person than when the contest or season began, convert us to new ways to see ourselves and our world. It should make us ask:

Is God present here on the field of play?

What does God expect of me in this contest?

What does God expect of me as a spectator?

Does this game enable me to see God in others on our team?

Does this game enable me to see God in our opponent?

Am I a better person for having played this game?

Am I a better person for having watched this game?

What does this game teach me about myself?

What does this game teach me about others?

Has this game helped me grow and change for the better?

Have I helped others on the team grow and change for the better?

Has this game helped make this a better community?

Can I be humble in victory and proud in defeat?

The moment of re-creation

Sister and brother athletes, the questions above are furthest from your mind as you set foot on the field of play, in the game, or recover from it. At those times, your mind and body must be solely on the game at hand — as carpenter, potter, painter, sculptor, and weaver are intent in their craft, their faces "set like flint" (Isaiah 50:7), absorbed in the task. Rather, you are to ask these questions in random moments when there is time to meditate, well before and well after the game.

What scoreboard cannot measure

The scoreboard never tells the whole story. It simply shows how many points each team scored, a numeric abstract. It cannot measure the courage, discipline, and selflessness of any team or its members. Sometimes the winner is the loser. Sometimes the loser is the winner.

"Sports at Saint John's were a great classroom where I learned at least two important life lessons. First, I learned sports are not to be the center of my life. You need balance. We were taught to focus, work as a team, play hard, but many other things in life matter more than sports. Second, I learned how to prepare for adversity. When you're in that locker room before the game, getting ready to go out onto the field, you don't know what's ahead. Good things can happen. Bad things can happen. You have to be ready to accept what comes at you and adjust to it."

Mike Grant
SJU, 1979

IX.
Moderation

We are content with living simply and frugally,
finding balance in work, prayer, and recreation.

"All things are done in moderation."
RB 48.9

Coaches should "regulate and arrange all matters" for their teams to ensure discipline, training, and teamwork. Athletes and coaches, however, should maintain a healthy balance in their lives and not make sports their overwhelming focus or be obsessed with external measures of self-worth. Players should be moderate in diet and nutrition, conditioning, lifting weights, and in running distances.

Harm of excessive training

Coaches should not impose on their players any training or practice harsh, burdensome, or "to the point of excess" — for as Jacob of the Old Testament is quoted in the Rule, "If I drive my flock too hard, they will all die in a single day." Coaches should take care: Don't burden your players with verbose speech, for "it is not in saying a great deal we shall be heard."

Moderating emotions

Athletes should leave any negative emotion from the game behind and not let it affect their relations with others on or off the field. Athletes in contact sports likewise should leave their hitting on the field and not be tempted to physically or verbally harm anyone.

Avoiding "self-exaltation"

Athletes should not be "inflated with pride" or "self-exaltation" or engage in any antics, associated with that of a circus, on the field, court, or rink that seek to attract attention to themselves at the expense of the team. Their focus should be on precisely executing plays on the field and their attitude one of humility. For example, in basketball, what is the purpose of the "slam" after a "dunk" except to draw attention to oneself at the expense of the team?

That spectators temper their zeal

Spectators are naturally passionate but must know the difference between the two "zeals" — the "zeal of bitterness" and the "good zeal." They show the "zeal of bitterness" when they chant to ridicule or harass. They show "good zeal" when they "loudly proclaim" for their team but not against the other team.

That spectators be not too quick to judge

Spectators should not be so consumed in the game that they later regret how they behaved in the heat of the moment. Their comments on the performance of a player should be phrased as if the player's parents were seated within hearing distance.

Monday morning quarterbacks: Be not too quick to chastise a coach or team for errors on the field or be "too ready to laugh" at a team's shortcomings. Have empathy for athletes who, in the midst of action on the field, must make decisions in a split second without benefit of a view of the entire field of play from above.

The intelligent spectator

Spectators should be discerning students of the game. They should know the rules of the game ("true and righteous altogether," Psalm 19:9) so they can correctly interpret actions by the coaches, players, and referees.

The physical well-being of spectators

Spectators should avoid wasting precious time watching too many games, in person or with remote devices (leaving them "remote" from the real world). They should devote at least as much time to their own physical well-being as to spectating. They should avoid wasting money on the Roman circus aspects of many commercial stadia such as luxury suites, drinking to excess, and prime seats that cost enough to feed a family of four for a month.

"Don Fischer, the head of our physical education department, modeled for me the Benedictine value of moderation — how he balanced family and work life. I knew him as the trainer, as assistant softball coach, as my kinesiology teacher, as a mentor, and family man. I even babysat his children. He helped develop my interest in sports medicine, and made it possible for me to explore the practice of orthopedic surgery. His passion for his family and his work made the Rule of Saint Benedict come to life for me."

Elena Jelsing
CSB, 2004

X.
Listening

We listen reverently with the ear of our heart
to all the voices of God's creation.

"Listen ... with the ear of your heart."
RB Prologue 1

The coach is accountable not just for the team's performance but its behavior. A coach should show players "all that is good and holy by his deeds even more than his words." He should "impose the same discipline on all" players and treat everyone fairly so that all "bear an equal burden of service." He should help players observe the rules of play, not circumvent them. Thus, players reflect in their behavior on the field the values of their coaches. A coach cannot be on the field with the players during the game, and so should convey to the players the knowledge, wisdom, and judgment needed to compete on the field as if the coach were not present.

The "ointment of encouragement"

Knowing there are a "variety of characters" on the team and that each player has different abilities and temperament, the coach — with "stern countenance and loving affection" — should be free to "reprove, entreat, rebuke" as the situation requires and to be "threatening at one time and coaxing at another as the occasion may require." Coaches should use the "ointment of encouragement." If a team is "rather large" in number, the coach "should be given helpers" in the form of assistant coaches, but they should not be an excessive entourage lest players be coached excessively, and thus not able to teach each other and to learn through their own trial and error.

Coaches listen to their players
Coaches must listen to athletes, entrusted to their care, with "attentive ears" to be attuned to each player's abilities and their physical and emotional limits.

Players listen to their coaches
Athletes must listen to their coaches and accept their guidance. Members of the team who are "undisciplined and restless" or who act in a "slovenly and careless way" must be "reproved rather sharply." Any lack of discipline or failure to observe the rules on the part of any player should be cut out "at the roots" immediately.

Players listen to their bodies
Athletes must listen to their bodies. They must know when to rest, when to push forward, when to seek medical care, when to cease play until the body can heal. When a body is out of harmony with the mind and the spirit, it is in discord.

Players listen to their consciences

Athletes must listen to their consciences and know right from wrong. In golf, count every stroke. In hockey, not use the stick as a weapon. In baseball and softball, not deliberately throw at the batter. In tennis, be fair in declaring when a ball is in or out of bounds. In wrestling, avoid illegal or life-threatening holds that cause an opponent to withdraw by suffering. In soccer, not slide into an opponent to free the ball with intent to injure. In volleyball, call a "touch" if the ball hits you before it goes out of bounds. Avoid deliberately hitting a player in any sport after the whistle is blown.

Sportswriters, broadcasters listen to their consciences

Sportswriters and broadcasters should be fair, accurate, and independent in their judgments, not beholden to either side but to the truth as they see it. Their descriptions and opinions reflect the values of the culture but also influence the shaping of those values, for good and ill. They should not describe certain games as "grudge matches" or attribute to any team a desire for "revenge" against another team. They should not stereotype athletes or teams based on their physical appearance, focus on a game's violence, or incite fans to riot.

"When you play Division III sports, you do it purely for the love of the game as a true amateur, not for athletic scholarships or money. What was most important to me was how we worked together as a team as part of a community, to achieve a common goal and share all the excitement, the disappointments, and the joy that were part of that journey. Contributing to the success of the team was a greater reward for me than any individual accomplishment."

Jennifer Nash-Wright
CSB, 1986

XI.
Common Good

We are committed to the good of the community
and respect for the individual.

"We intend to establish a school for the Lord's service …
We hope to set down nothing harsh, nothing burdensome.
The good of all concerned may prompt us to a little
strictness in order to amend faults and to safeguard love."
RB Prologue 45–47

It's human nature to keep records of individual achievement in sports — the longest run, the most hits, catches, goals — even to enshrine individual performance in "halls of fame." Measuring just one player's performance, however, not only can make that performance a commodity but can diminish the common good of the team. Therefore, the team's record is more important than any one player's performance. Football players, for example, should avoid displaying any symbols of individual achievement on their helmets or jerseys.

Unselfish assistance

Each player has a position on the field, court, or rink and is given certain responsibilities. This narrow responsibility, however, is not as important as each player's responsibility for the good of the team. A player who, through a timely block or feint, unselfishly assists the success of a play makes as important a contribution as the player who carries the ball or scores the points.

All positions on the team valued

All positions on the team are of equal importance to the team's success; each has "a part to play in the whole" (1 Corinthians 12:27).

No position should be described as a "skill" position; for are we then to call other positions "unskilled" and are they, thus, inferior?

Competition for positions

There is a finite number of positions for any sport — five on the court, six on the rink, nine on the diamond, 11 on the gridiron, or pitch. Those who compete for the same position know only one can be chosen and should support each other, without jealousy or envy, and respect the coach's choice for the greater good of the team.

Accepting victory or defeat

The true "hero" accepts victory or defeat with grace. Accepting defeat can transform the player, thereby preparing one to accept much more painful losses later in life.

"Moral victory"

If there be a "moral victory," the consolation of almost defeating a superior opponent, then there also can be a "moral defeat," the consolation of barely losing to an inferior opponent.

When deception may be used

Deceiving the opponent is an acceptable and desired tactic in sports as long as the rules of fair play are observed — such as "stealing" signs on the field, bluffing or faking as to where the ball will be thrown, hit, or carried, or in baseball when the runner tries to stop a double play by "taking out" a fielder. When deception and trickery are outside the rules and create unfair advantage, it's cheating, such as spitballs, corked bats, drug use, or trying to intimidate referees and umpires.

All "Number One" in God's eyes

Players and spectators chant "We're Number One!" after winning, but in God's eyes all who play fair in sports are "Number One." All teams should strive to achieve the excellence associated with being Number One, but not with boastful pride. If you're indeed "Number One," then the score is proof enough. As a wise coach said, you're never as good as everyone tells you when you win, and never as bad as they say when you lose.

"We had to fight for equal access to resources for sports and earn respect as athletes. We had to beg the campus security officer to let us use the gym after hours. The floor was linoleum on concrete, and there was one foot between the brick wall and the out-of-bounds line for basketball. We had to buy our own uniform shirts. We had volunteer refs for the eight to ten games we played, which were mostly scrimmages. We car-pooled to away games. I was the only one on campus who had sweatpants! But we did have fun, and we built lifelong friendships, and we laid the foundation for Saint Ben's sports today. That gives me great pride."

Nancy Frost Bellmont
CSB, 1974

XII.
Justice

We work toward a just order on our campuses and in our society.

"… that in all things may God be glorified."
RB 57.9

Since all are created equally in God's likeness, thus all should have equal opportunity to compete in athletics as far as their skill and determination can take them — female and male, whatever color or creed, or if limited in the use of their bodies.

Inside and outside the walls

There should be just distribution of resources for all who seek to play, whether on teams that compete "inside the walls" of the campus (*intramural*) or on teams that compete against other schools "outside the walls" (*extramural*). Since few students have the talent and skill for intercollegiate sports, there should be enough resources available for the many more who play intramural or club sports. Since the "wall" doesn't exist in God's eyes, achievement on the field, court, or rink inside the walls by the athlete of average ability is no less valuable than the prowess of the athlete who competes outside the walls.

Rules of the game

Games have rules so standards of fairness are enforced, so the boundaries of play are defined, so those who do not observe the rules are penalized. "If one takes part in an athletic contest," wrote

Saint Paul (2 Timothy 2:5), "he cannot receive the winner's crown unless he has kept the rules."

Principles versus rules

What's said about ethics in business applies to sports. If athletes value and observe the principles of fair play, they'll have no trouble following the rules of the game. Rules are the letter of the game, principles the spirit. Rules tell a player what to decide, principles how to decide. Rules change, principles endure. Rules are specific, principles universal. Rules are complex, easily "gamed"; principles are simple.

The role of the referee

All should respect the judgments of the referees (*re-ferre*, Latin, to bring back), appointed by both teams to discern and administer the rules with fairness and maintain the game's orderly flow. The referee should allow players to compete within the spirit and intent of the rules and penalize players and coaches who break the rules.

Players and coaches should see referees as "custodians of trust" for the rules, not border guards to be eluded through trickery. A player or coach who believes it's cheating only if caught — such as teaching players to illegally hold or push a competitor or to pretend to be injured to stop play — has no place in sports. There's a difference, as sportswriter Frank Deford notes, between sportsmanship and gamesmanship. Indeed, he points out: The game most known for sportsmanship, golf, is the only one in which the players are their own referees.

Referee must earn respect

Referees deserve respect. Regardless of the final score, they should be thanked for their contributions. To deserve respect, a referee should not be officious or dictatorial but should assume the best of coaches and athletes.

What a referee should do

A referee should:

- understand the spirit and intent of each rule to apply it judiciously — since there can't be a rule for every conceivable situation,

- ensure no player or team has an unfair advantage,

- be consistent in interpreting rules and applying judgment so as not to be arbitrary,

- adjust to the level of skill and behavior of the players,
- ensure tempers are under control if the quality of play or behavior deteriorates,
- not wager on games or be connected with gambling in any way,
- not ignore any obvious violation of a rule, and
- listen as patiently as possible to a coach's complaint.

Abundant rules

The conduct of a player or team is governed by abundant rules to penalize them for what they should *not* do — yellow cards and red cards, penalty kicks, penalty boxes, ejections after five personal fouls, 15-yard penalties, or "downs" deprived. Players and teams, however, are accorded no similar advantages on the field for fair play. Therefore, players should monitor their own behavior and let it be its own reward.

Epilogue: Time to Play!

Benedict lays down his pen. Thesis done. His dorm window gives off a solitary glow in the winter night. The bells of the Abbey church bong across the snow-drifted campus. It is 1 a.m. Time for bed.

His cell phone chimes a text message.

Benno. RU up? How bout BB in Palaestra?

He stretches his stiffened legs, palms his eyes to rub out the tiredness. He thumbs a response:

Could use xrcise. Be right over! IOGD* Thx.

* *In omnibus glorificetur Deus (In all things may God be glorified.)*

Contributors

Spanning more than a half century of athletics at Saint Ben's and Saint John's

Nancy Frost Bellmont, 1974, majored in social work and was a member of the first CSB basketball team in 1972–73. She was one of two CSB student representatives to attend a state-wide meeting in the early 1970s to discuss the future of women's college athletics. She is a probation officer in Stearns County (Minn.).

Grace Donovan, *O.S.B.*, played basketball in high school in the 1940s when it was simply halftime entertainment during boys' games. She received degrees in physical education and history from the University of Wisconsin (LaCrosse), a master's in history from St. Louis University (Mo.), and helped build intramurals and intercollegiate sports at CSB. She is the retired head of aging services for Catholic Charities of St. Cloud (Minn.).

Mike Grant, 1979, majored in social science and was a member of the 1976 national championship SJU football team. He has been football coach at Eden Prairie High School (Minn.) since 1992 and athletic director since 2002. His football teams have won five state championships.

Adam Hanna, 2006, Owatonna (Minn.), majored in economics and was starting SJU hockey goalie for three seasons. He set school records for the lowest goals-against average, highest save percentage, and most shutouts, and was named the nation's outstanding Division III hockey player in 2006. He plays goalie for the Bossier City (La.) team in the Central Hockey League.

Margaret Hughes has degrees in physical education from the University of Minnesota (B.S.) and Saint Cloud State (M.A.). She chaired the CSB physical education department, helped CSB join the Minnesota Intercollegiate Athletic Conference (MIAC) in 1985, and introduced the coaching certification program. She is retired, a professor emerita in physical education at CSB.

Elena "Ellie" Jelsing, 2004, majored in natural science, played varsity CSB soccer two years, varsity softball four years, received the Scholar-Athlete Award as a senior and a post-graduate NCAA scholarship. In 2004 she was part of a mission team that provided free medical services in Haiti. She is a medical student at Mayo Medical School (Rochester, Minn.).

Daniel Kramer, *Ph.D.*, 1989, majored in English, philosophy, and European humanities, and competed in SJU cross country and track and field (400-meter hurdles, mile relay). He received his M.A. in comparative literature from the University of Wisconsin (Madison), his Ph.D. from Harvard, was a Fulbright teaching assistant, and is an assistant professor of German at Washington and Lee University, Lexington (Va.).

Jim Lehman, 1956, majored in social studies, and played SJU football, basketball, and baseball. In 1955 he averaged 117 yards a game rushing and became the first SJU running back to rush for more than 1,000 yards in a season. His 1955 average of 8.1 yards a carry remains a school record more than 50 years later. He was conference MVP his senior year. He is a retired insurance sales executive from Alexandria (Minn.).

Joe Mucha, 1966, majored in history, played basketball and football, and was a member of both the 1963 and 1965 SJU national championship football teams. He is a retired vice president of human resources at General Mills, Inc. (Minneapolis) and a member of the Saint John's Board of Regents.

Jennifer Nash-Wright, Ph.D., 1986, majored in theology with a minor in secondary education, was the most valuable player and all-conference in basketball for 1983–1985, and was the first CSB player to score more than 1,000 points in her career. She has a master's degree in psychology (Saint Mary's University, Winona, Minn.), a doctorate in clinical psychology (Argosy University, Eagan, Minn.), and a private practice in St. Louis Park (Minn.).

Dr. Chris Palmer, M.D., 1996, majored in biology and played baseball and football. He was an All-American in SJU football in 1994 and 1995 and was awarded the Gagliardi Trophy as the nation's Outstanding Division III football player for excellence in athletics, academics, and community service. He is an emergency room physician at North Memorial Regional Hospital in Robbinsdale (Minn.).

Kathy Yarnott Lowry, 1992, majored in nursing, was a soccer goalie four years, and a member of the first CSB team to compete in the NCAA Championships (1990). She was the nation's Goalkeeper of the Year, an All-American, and recipient of the All-American Scholar Collegiate Award. She is a U.S. Air Force major, graduate of the Squadron Officer School (ranking second among 702 students), and provided medical care for troops in the former Yugoslavia in 1995 and in Kosovo and Macedonia in 2000. She is stationed at Travis Air Force Base (Calif.).

Some Reading

Araton, Harvey. *Alive and Kicking: When Soccer Moms Take the Field and Change Their Lives Forever.* New York: Simon & Schuster, 2001.

Branch, John. "Rodriguez Keeps Straddling Baseball's Foul Line," *The New York Times*, June 1, 2007.

Clemens, Teri. *Get With It, Girls! Life Is Competition.* Diamond Communications, 2001.

Cooper, Cynthia. *She Got Game: My Personal Odyssey.* New York: Warner Books, 2000.

Cox, Lynne. *Swimming to Antarctica.* New York: Knopf, 2004.

Dowling, Colette. *The Frailty Myth: Redefining the Physical Potential of Women and Girls.* New York: Random House USA, 2002.

Ford, Gerald R. with John Underwood. "My View of Sport," *Sports Illustrated*, July 8, 1974.

Gallico, Paul. *Farewell to Sport.* New York: Alfred A. Knopf, 1938.

Higgs, Robert. *God in the Stadium: Sports and Religion in America.* Lexington: University Press of Kentucky, 1995.

Holmes, Arthur. *Contours of a World View.* Grand Rapids, Mich.: Eerdmans, 1983.

Lasch, Christopher. "The Corruption of Sports," *The New York Review of Books*, 24:7. April 28, 1977.

Longman, Jere. *The Girls of Summer: The U.S. Women's Soccer Team and How It Changed the World.* Scranton, Pa.: HarperCollins Publishers, 2000.

Lutter, Judy Mahle. *Of Heroes, Hopes and Level Playing Fields.* Saint Paul, Minn., Melpomene Institute, 1996.

McCarthy, Eugene. "A Copenhagen Snuff Can Filled with Dirt," *Hockey* magazine, March 1978.

Miller, Stephen. *Arête: Greek Sports from Ancient Sources.* Berkeley: University of California Press, 1991.

Nelson, Mariah Burton. *We Are All Athletes.* Dare Press, 2002.

Novak, Michael. *The Joy of Sports: Endzones, Bases, Baskets, Balls, and the Consecration of the American Spirit.* London: Hamilton Press, 1988 (1967).

Rice, Grantland. *Only the Brave and Other Poems.* A.S. Barnes and Co., 1941.

Sheehan, George. *Running and Being.* New York: Simon & Schuster, 1978.

Simon, Robert L. *Fair Play: The Ethics of Sport.* Boulder, Colo.: Westview Press, 2003.

Sperber, Murray. *Beer and Circus: How Big-Time College Sports Is Crippling Undergraduate Education.* New York: Henry Holt & Co., 2000.

Storey, David. *This Sporting Life.* London: Longmans, 1960.

Summit, Pat. *Reach for the Summit.* New York: Broadway Books, 1998.

Turner, Philip. "For some, exercise jogs spirituality," Religion News Service, *Star Tribune* (Minneapolis), June 16, 2007, E10.

Weiss, Paul. *Sport: A Philosophic Inquiry.* Carbondale, Ill.: Southern Illinois University Press, 1969.

Zumsteg, Derek. *The Cheater's Guide to Baseball.* Boston: Houghton Mifflin, 2007.

The Canadian Amateur Wrestling Association:
http://www.wrestling.ca/coaches/code_of_ethics.php

Canadian Ministers of Sport:
truesportpur.ca/files/Secretariat/Documents/FPT-CCES-
LondonDeclaration-E.pdf

Institute on College Student Values:
collegevalues.org/proceedings.cfm?ID=11

Institute for International Sport:
internationalsport.com

Referee Enterprises, Inc.:
www.referee.com/sampleArticles

Sports Illustrated:
sportsillustrated.cnn.com/inside_game/archives/frank_deford

Acknowledgments

Among those who enriched this little effort directly or indirectly:

Abbot John Klassen, O.S.B., Carol Howe-Veenstra, Tom Stock, Thom Woodward, Lee Hanley, Daniel Durken, O.S.B., Janna LaFountaine, Timothy Backous, O.S.B., Hilary Thimmesh, O.S.B., Don Talafous, O.S.B., Eric Hollas, O.S.B., Lois Wedl, O.S.B., Colman O'Connell, O.S.B., Emmanuel Renner, O.S.B., Johnny Thompson, Jon McGee, Mary Geller, Gar Kellom, Pat McDonnell, Roger Hipwell, Bernie Weber, Fred Cremer, Mike Scherer, Tom Gillham, John Ford, Drake Dierkhising, Dan Fazendin, Peter Stoddart, Mike Williams, Christopher Williams, Rich Chalmers, John Rogers, Monica Little, Mike Schacherer, Sheree Mehring, Chris Heimbold, Frank Schmidt, Tim Schumann, Mary Haeg, Daniel Haeg, Emily and John Saunders, Mary and Andrew Haeg, Angela and Peter Haeg, Fritz Haeg, and Maggie Hogan.